A Pin

Written by Caroline Green

Illustrated by Marusha Belle

Collins

sit

· · ·

pin

3

sit

pin

nap

pat

nap

pat

tap

sip

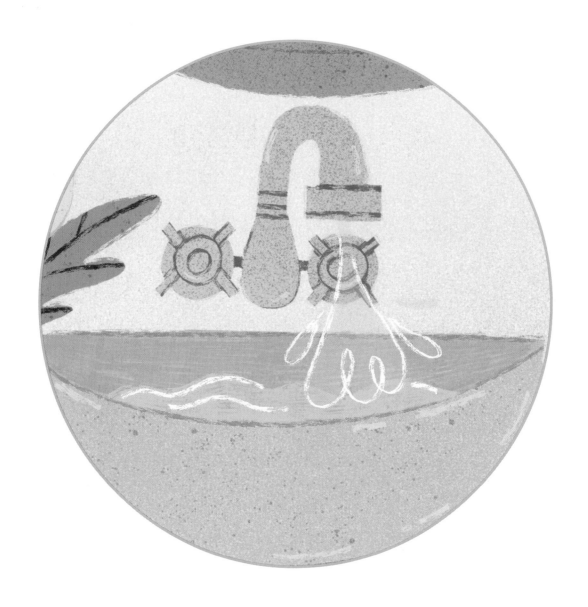

tap

sip

/p/

14

15

🐾 Review: After reading 🐾

Use your assessment from hearing the children read to choose any words that need additional practice.

Read 1: Decoding

- Say the sounds in the words below.
- Ask the children to repeat the sounds and then say the word.

  s/i/t **sit**   s/i/p **sip**   p/a/t **pat**   p/i/n **pin**   t/a/p **tap**

- If the children cannot work out what a word is, say the sounds, and then say the word. Tell the children to repeat after you.
- Look at the "I spy sounds" pages (14–15) and ask the children to look for items in the picture that use the /p/ sound. (*pear, plums, purple, pink, pigeon, peacocks, pin, plate, pillows, pattern*)

Read 2: Prosody

- Model reading each word with expression to the children. After you have read the story, ask the children to have a go at reading with expression.
- Make a chant using the words in the story by repeating them three times. Encourage the children to chant the words in different ways: quietly for "nap, nap, nap" and loudly or urgently for "pat, pat, pat".

Read 3: Comprehension

- Go back through the book and discuss the pictures. Encourage children to talk about details that stand out for them. Use a dialogic talk model to expand on their ideas and recast them in full sentences as naturally as possible.
- Work together to expand vocabulary by naming objects in the pictures that children do not know.
- Ask the children:
  - What does the pin make the princess do? (*go to sleep*)
  - How does the princess wake up? (*the rabbit pats her*)
  - What does she sip? (*water from the tap*)
- Ask the children if they know of a story where these things happen (*Sleeping Beauty*). What do they know about the story?